MARK & DIANE BUTTON

The Letter Box

A Story of Enduring Love

Manjul Publishing House

First published in India by

MANJUL

Manjul Publishing House Pvt. Ltd.,
10, Nishat Colony, Bhopal, INDIA - 462 003
Ph.: +91 755 424 0340 Fax: +91 755 405 5791
E-mail: manjul@manjulindia.com
Website : www.manjulindia.com

First published: 2009

First published by Beyond Words Publishing, Inc., Hillsboro, Oregon.
www.beyondword.com. All rights reserved. English translation rights arranged
through Sylvia Hayse Literary Agency, LLC, Bandon, Oregon USA.

ISBN   978 - 81 - 8322 - 139 - 9

Editor: Jenefer Angell
Managing editor: Julie Steigerwaldt
Proofreader: Marvin Moore
Design: AutHaus
Composition: William H. Brunson Typography Services

The hand lettering in the title and part openers was specially created for
The Letter Box by Clint Gorthy.

Printed & bound in India by
Thomson Press (India) Ltd.

THIS BOOK IS DEDICATED TO

RONNIE LEW BUTTON

who gave us the inspiration
to celebrate life each day, to cherish our family,
and to record our journey,
however short or long it may prove to be.

PART ONE

The Letter Box

1

PART TWO

Your Own Letter Box

111

ACKNOWLEDGMENTS

143

The Letter Box

PART ONE

IT HAS BEEN OVER A YEAR OF CRUNCHING numbers, flying back and forth across the country, and late-night meetings with lawyers and accountants. My wife, Ronnie, and I have considered our future and how our lives will change if this deal actually happens. With my mind so focused, I have hardly taken the time to understand the emotional investment of this negotiation.

Almost everyone who my partner, Scott Stillinger, and I really care about has supported our decision to sell the business, including our upper-management team. We have all worked hard and been through so much together, yet we are ready to move on.

In terms of success and my career, I have proven myself to myself and to those who are important to me. Now I want to prove myself in other areas. I want to sit with Ronnie on our porch in Hawaii, watch the sunrise, and appreciate it completely. God only knows how many times I have sat alone in my California office and not even looked out the window for an entire day. I have been preoccupied—too busy to really be still. I wonder if I have ever truly appreciated a beautiful sunset. Success has its rewards, but I have missed out in other ways.

With the simple stroke of a pen, I knew I could win financial security for my future family and provide us the ability to live and fully enjoy our lives and each other. I don't often find myself feeling nervous or anxious, but the moment we stepped into the elevator and pushed the button to take us to the thirty-eighth floor, something hit me: All the years of my life had brought me to this one pivotal moment.

The original idea for the product had come from Scott. It seemed a reasonable gamble to me: a ball that would make it easy for kids to learn how to catch. I knew from experience that success in the toy industry doesn't follow the path of adult logic. Yet there was something extra and indefinable about this. We decided on the name "Koosh Ball" and described it as "easy to catch and hard to put down." The first obstacle was that neither we, nor anyone else, knew how to manufacture it. Therefore, we didn't know how much it would cost, what it would look like, what it should sell for, or if anyone would even like it.

At the time, many of our friends and family thought we were crazy. They made comments like "I can't believe you're going to quit your jobs for a ball made out of rubber bands." We put our life savings on the line in an effort to prove them wrong. We left our secure jobs, rented an old converted barn in Silicon Valley, and started our business, OddzOn Products, Inc. Despite the odds, our first Koosh Balls were shipped only six months later—a miracle in itself. So began our decade-long obsession with colorful rubber bands. The rest became history in a quick uphill climb toward the top of the toy-industry charts.

It had been an exciting time, filled with good products, great friendships, and rapid sales growth. Like all success-ful start-ups, the company had taken on a life of its own. But after several years, I began to take a serious look at my life and priorities. The point of our business venture was to have fun and make money—with the ultimate goal of having more time and freedom. It's amazing how easy it is to become consumed by something that provides mostly money, even though money is supposed to be only the tool to reach the higher causes.

Now, with products sold all around the world, we were about to sell the company and achieve even more success than I had ever imagined. Scott and our attorney, Jeff Kramer, seemed relaxed and at ease. We were as prepared as we could possibly be. I took a deep breath and stepped into what would be the longest and most memorable meeting of my career.

Ten people were sitting along one side of a long, dark table in an air-conditioned conference room. I was thankful the gratuitous small talk was short-lived. Within minutes we were in a serious contract negotiation.

The number of people we were dealing with surprised me. They had ten—but we had Jeff, a man with more credentials following his name than any other person I have ever known. We didn't need an army to help us; we had him. We were ready to roll.

Our Thursday-morning meeting continued on into the evening. Both sides agreed to keep going. We had come too far. We weren't planning to leave until this was finished, one way or another. We went back and forth over every point. We watched the sun come up over Manhattan through the conference-room windows. The view was magnificent.

On a couple of occasions, I thought we would have to walk away from the table. It was tense. As we were going over the final details, it seemed obvious they were stalling. It was now Friday afternoon, and it seemed clear they wanted to hold up the timing until next week, which was the beginning of a new quarter. Or maybe they just wanted the interest over the weekend.

I have never seen Jeff lose his temper or even raise his voice, but I could see he was getting frustrated. He was cautious because he had our future at stake, but he was firm.

Jeff had asked the lawyers several times to insert a small but critical clause into our contract. They had agreed, but each time it came back for us to review, it was incorrect.

Finally I leaned over to a senior lawyer, handed him a piece of paper, and said, "The language has to be just like this, exactly like this, and not any different. If it doesn't come back exactly like this, we won't close this deal. If we don't close this deal by the end of the day, we're not doing it on Monday. Got it?"

I sat back and held my breath.

The corrections were made; we signed the contract and waited at the office until we received confirmation that the wire transfer had come through. OddzOn Products, Inc., and all its Koosh-brand products were now the property of someone else. We finally left the office and, I must say, the elevator ride down was a lot more fun than going up had been.

When I returned to California, Ronnie was waiting for me at the airport. We hugged tightly, looked at each other, and smiled that magical, deep smile of common amazement. We wanted to celebrate, but more importantly, we realized that our lives had just changed in ways we couldn't yet begin to understand.

SPRING

To some of my friends and casual acquaintances, I may appear unsentimental, but this is not the case at all. I savor traditions and I love deeply. No one knows this more than my wife of almost eight years, Ronnie Lew.

True, I don't often lavish her with expensive gifts, but I have not yet missed an opportunity to celebrate our life and our love. Wedding anniversaries and birthdays do not slip by unnoticed in our house. Maybe the entire festivity entails only a simple card and a kiss, but she knows that my heart belongs to her alone.

We both love to sail, and we have discovered that a compass, a rudder, a mast, or almost anything that has to do with sailing in the open sea can be a reflection of the wonder of life, a mirror into our very soul. Last Valentine's Day my card was a metaphor of sorts:

Ronnie Lew,

You are the wind,
and the stars,
my compass and
my helm.

Unfurl my sails.
Guide my way.
Help me
to be the best
I can be.

*Fill my life with
your fullness ... and
let our love spill
over for others to
see.*

Forever, Mark

The day I proposed to Ronnie, I promised her that we would someday build our own house and fill it with as many children as she wanted. We also hoped to travel and see some other places in the world. Many of these dreams have already come true. On our first vacation after our honeymoon, we stumbled upon a magical spot on the North Shore of Oahu. One breezy afternoon we were relaxing in Adirondack chairs underneath a palm tree listening to the ocean. I had just come in from surfing, and I was feeling completely at peace with our surroundings.

I looked around the quiet beachfront community and said to Ronnie, "This is good. I mean really good. We could live here."

"And it's a neighborhood," added Ronnie. "This could be a perfect place to raise our kids."

A year later we put in offers up and down the street. Nothing had sold in years, but eventually we were able to buy a small lot and build our dream home. All we needed to do was move to our house on the beach and fill it up with children.

M

We've already been trying to get pregnant for over four years, with no success. We've seen specialists at Stanford. We've tried fertility drugs. At the recommendation of an expert in San Francisco, we attempted in-vitro fertilization. It's been years filled with countless injections, disappointments, and tears.

Ronnie wants children more than anything else in life, and for that reason alone I think it may be time to consider adoption. I know it hurts her to hear me say that. She simply isn't ready to give up trying yet. It's not that we wouldn't immediately fall in love with any newborn baby. I don't want to push her, but the adoption attorneys say it could take up to a year. Ronnie wants to give in-vitro one more try, so I have agreed to that, but I've suggested that we move forward with the adoption paperwork as well.

Once again, seeing Ronnie's eggs fertilized in a dish was anything but romantic, but for us they mean hope. And despite the clinical trappings, this hope may in fact be our first emotional bond with our potential family.

We know from past experience that the insemination process causes slight discomfort. The doctors suggest listening to calming music during the procedure, but Ronnie wanted me to read to her from the book she's just started, *A Severe Mercy*, written by Sheldon Vanauken. Although it is a tragic story of a man who loses his beloved wife, it's so eloquently written that I felt like I was reading her a passionate love story. Even the doctor commented on how soothing it was.

Waiting for two long weeks after the insemination to go in for a pregnancy test has been tough. But it was worth the wait, because the news is good: positive—finally!

It's so exciting! Ronnie and I talk about boys versus girls, how our life together will change, and how happy we are.

This baby is an answered prayer. We've decided not to tell anyone yet. It's still early. Maybe after the next appointment, when the doctor confirms the news with an ultrasound, we can make the announcement to our family and friends.

When Ronnie's doctor did the ultrasound, we saw the baby's heart beating strongly—but as we looked closer at the image on the screen, we saw another heart beating too.

The doctor smiled at us and said, "Congratulations, you're having twins."

Our thrill at having twins is only exceeded by our relief at seeing those two heartbeats. We'd gotten to this stage before only to find that the little heart was not beating. This time, our dream is really coming true. A new generation is on the way.

I had a dream the other night that we already had three children, but I knew it was a dream because Ronnie and I didn't recognize them. It was an odd feeling because we seemed distant somehow, like we hadn't yet connected as a family. Besides, they all had blond hair, which is very unlikely, given Ronnie's dark hair and brown eyes. I can't help myself; now I keep teasing her that we are actually having three.

She always wants me to rub her tummy in this certain way. Sometimes I pretend to count the babies when I rub her stomach, and after I get to two, I pause to look at the smile on her face. She looks like an angel to me now. But then I can't resist, and after counting to two, I feel around a little bit more and finally say, "Three." She always laughs. It's so easy to make her laugh. I've always loved that about her.

(M)

During our routine checkup yesterday, the doctor said that some of our "numbers" were a bit higher than normal. He told us not to be alarmed, but he wanted to do another ultrasound just to be sure everything was progressing normally. After all we've been through, it was impossible not to worry.

He stared at the monitor, squinted his eyes, and wrinkled his forehead for a long time without speaking.

"Is everything all right?" Ronnie asked him, a bit nervously.

"I'm just taking a closer look. Don't worry, everything looks fine," he reassured us. Then he showed us what he was seeing.

Not only were both babies growing normally, but a third—an identical twin—was there as well.

"Oh my, triplets!" Ronnie beamed.

We couldn't believe it. This was by far the happiest moment of our life together. Here was the large family we had been dreaming about for so many years.

The doctor and nurses stepped out to give us a minute alone. I didn't really even think of needing a minute alone until they left. I looked at Ronnie, and her smile just grew and grew. She looked at me so sweetly and just said, "Three." We hugged, and I felt myself welling up with tears. Finally these were the good kind of tears. We were going to be the proud parents of triplets!

We left the clinic overjoyed. On our way home, as we drove across the Golden Gate Bridge, I looked over and saw that Ronnie had the giggles.

"What's so funny?" I asked her.

Between the laughter she looked over at me and said, "I think God has an incredible sense of humor."

Later that day, I was standing in the front yard when my best friend, Dave, drove up and parked in my driveway. I must have looked like a child on a pogo stick, jumping up and down with excitement.

"What's up with you?" he asked.

"There's three!" I cheered.

"Three what? Three—no way. Don't tell me." Dave looked stunned.

"Yep. We're having triplets!" I smiled proudly.

"You have no idea what you're in store for. Just wait, you have no idea." Dave was smiling, but he was obviously not as wildly ecstatic to hear the news as I was to tell it. He knows from experience how much energy it takes to raise three children, not to mention three in diapers.

Dave laughed and went on, "Well, congratulations. Your life is going to change more than you could ever imagine."

He is such a realist.

I've never seen Ronnie enjoy being the center of attention, but she definitely enjoyed every minute of it this past week in Phoenix. She was the talk of the town. Our friends at the Toy Manufacturers of America meeting were spreading the news that we were expecting triplets, and Ronnie was just glowing. Friends were there from around the country, and it was so special for us to get to share the news with everyone in person.

Though officially out of the toy business, I still found myself in meetings most of the day. While I was busy, Ronnie took advantage of her free time by going to the health spa. She also relaxed with her friends and took some leisurely desert trail hikes.

The doctors have told her to take it easy during the first trimester, so she joked that she would forego horseback riding for now. She got a bit of a headache on Tuesday— probably from all the excitement. She just rested quietly that afternoon, and we flew home this morning.

In terms of both business and pleasure, it was a fabulous trip. Who says you can't have it all? I can't imagine life could get much better than this.

On the ninth of May, just a few days from Mother's Day, Ronnie rolled over and snuggled into my arms. She nudged me softly and whispered, "Do you realize that next year on Mother's Day three bouncing babies will be climbing into our bed?"

I have never seen her so happy.

Ronnie left for a doctor's appointment around ten o'clock. I hadn't been feeling well, so I stayed home. I was resting in bed and reading when the phone rang. The doctor was on the line and said that my wife was in the office and that she was complaining of a severe headache.

I spoke briefly to Ronnie and she asked if I could come and get her. I grabbed my keys and drove to the doctor's office to pick her up.

As I pulled up to the clinic, I saw an ambulance in front and lots of activity. Two paramedics were rushing into the building with a stretcher. I went down the street and parked to stay away from the commotion, but as I entered the building I realized the paramedics were there for Ronnie. I ran to her side and told her not to worry, that I loved her, and that we would take care of this. Still, I had no idea what was going on, but she looked as if her head was throbbing, and she seemed to be dizzy.

I jumped in my car and followed the ambulance, speeding behind it all the way to the hospital. The drive seemed to take forever, like a slow-motion movie. I wondered if the triplets were in jeopardy. Ronnie had already had two miscarriages, and I knew that losing these babies would devastate her.

I prayed.

When we finally made it to the hospital, I ran to the ambulance to see Ronnie. I could tell immediately that her condition had worsened. She seemed to be only partially aware of her surroundings, and I was beginning to get frightened. I tried to calm her by telling her that everything would be fine, but I'm afraid that my own fear was impossible to hide.

I called Dave, and within half an hour he was there. It was about that time the doctor came out to talk to me. I sat stunned as he told me the news. Ronnie had a brain aneurysm and needed to get to surgery as soon as possible. It had nothing to do with the triplets or a miscarriage. It was much more serious than I had ever imagined.

The wait was an eternity. The doctor assured me that Ronnie was in the best possible hands and that everything would be done to care for her and to protect the lives of the triplets. That made me feel better for a while.

By the time the surgery was completed it was late evening and I was surrounded by several of my friends and family. The doctor said the surgery went well, but we would need to wait until morning to be certain there was no permanent damage. They gave me five minutes to go in and see her. Her head was wrapped in bandages, so I couldn't kiss her face. I sat and held her hand instead. She was breathing with the help of a machine and appeared to be sound asleep. I wasn't allowed to stay with her too long; she needed rest and quiet. The doctor and nurses encouraged me to go home and get some sleep, and they promised to call if there were any changes in her condition. I reluctantly went home to try to get some sleep.

Before dawn I was on my way back to the hospital, feeling positive because I didn't get a call during the night. I expected to walk into Ronnie's room and be greeted with a groggy smile, but I soon found out that wasn't the situation at all. The doctor looked solemnly at me. He was noticeably uneasy as he told me that Ronnie had never regained consciousness. He said he was sorry to have to tell me that she was brain-dead and that soon they should take her off life support. There was nothing more they could do for her.

My world was slowly coming to a stop. I saw people talking all around me, but I could not make sense of what they were saying. A woman with the doctor was reminding me that Ronnie had signed an organ-donor card years before. My eyes blurred, yet I could see them going about their business in a practiced way. Ronnie's liver would fail soon and time was of the essence. I was told that she was gone and that I was going to lose the triplets, too.

I couldn't accept those words. I wouldn't allow them to take Ronnie off life support. I needed time. With the help of my closest and most resourceful friends, we called every place we possibly could to find out if anything could be done to save them.

It was soon clear that Ronnie was not coming back. At times it seemed there might be hope for the triplets, but in the end we learned that they were too young. It had never been done before. It was impossible.

My friends and family went in to say their good-byes to Ronnie. Dozens of people were gathered in the waiting room. I went in last and sat by her side. I held her hand, told her I loved her, and recited our wedding vows. There were no other words. I left the room, and the life-support system was removed. Ronnie and the babies died at 3:05 P.M. on Sunday afternoon. It was May 12. Mother's Day.

I can't recall how I made it home from the hospital, although I am certain I didn't drive. All I can remember is the unbearable sadness I felt climbing into bed alone that first night.

Days have been a blur. Dave and many other close friends have virtually taken over my life, including making plans for the funeral and all of the details that seem so surreal yet so final. It's all too much for me to believe. Life has rendered me empty and vulnerable.

There are no words that can possibly console me, though everybody has tried. My close friend Jamie, who flew out to be with me as soon as he heard the news, did tell me one story that gave me some small comfort. It's from *A Man Called Peter*, a movie about Peter Marshall, a former chaplain for the United States Senate. In the movie, Peter Marshall gives a sermon about a young boy who is dying of a terminal illness. One night the boy asks his mother, "Mommy, what happens when you die?"

Jamie explained that the mother wants to be truthful but also wants her son to be comforted as much as possible. She tells the little boy that it is like when he falls asleep on the couch at night and his daddy picks him up in his big, strong arms and carries him upstairs. He gets tucked into bed, kissed goodnight, and later he wakes up in his own room.

I knew he was right. I knew that the same thing had happened to Ronnie. She had fallen asleep in a soft, cozy bed, and God had picked her up in His strong arms and carried her home. When Ronnie was alive, we had almost everything one could desire on earth. Now I believe she has much more—but I have lost everything.

M

I want her back. No, I want to go with her and the children. What could possibly be left for me here without them?

My body aches. My lungs fill with unwanted air and my heart beats against its own will. I feel lost. No amount of sleep will wake me from this nightmare. The doctors say I'm healthy. They poke and prod the shell of a man. The real me is not here. The real me has gone.

I've had a wonderful life. I was blessed with a beautiful wife. I've made more money than I am likely to spend. Of course, the money is meaningless now; it can't turn back the clock. It doesn't ease the pain in my heart or help me to sleep. I guess I'm just waiting now—waiting for an end to my suffering.

When Ronnie had gotten on the phone that morning at the doctor's office, her voice was so soft and apologetic: "Sweetheart, can you come pick me up? I really need you." I had no way of knowing it would be one of the "snapshot memories" the psychiatrists warned me about. I had no way of knowing she was already leaving me behind. I had no time to tell her, "No! Don't leave me. It is I who really needs you."

All that I feel now is the pain.

M

There is no silver lining here. Right now it's all just too real. Dave called me this morning asking what I wanted Ronnie's headstone to say.

"How about 'Ronnie Lew Button, loving wife'?" I paused a moment to consider the option of using her legal and more formal name, Veronica.

"That's perfect, Mark, and so true. Do you want to include the dates of her birth and death?" This was Dave's way of making sure the final decision was indeed mine.

What I really wanted it to say was "Ronnie Lew Button, the most amazing loving wife of eight years, thoughtful and sincere friend who was always there for anyone, excellent and creative photographer of bizarre objects, avid reader, and lover of flowers of all kinds who dreamed of lots of happy children running around her house."

"Yes, Ronnie Lew Button, a loving wife, December 9, 1957, to May 12, 1996." I still couldn't believe I was saying those words.

I hung up the phone and thought to myself, "Mother's Day. What an unbelievable twist of fate that Ronnie should die on the very holiday she most dreamed of celebrating."

I called Dave back. "I've changed my mind about the headstone. What I want it to say is 'Ronnie Lew Button, a loving wife, mother, and friend' and then the dates underneath."

Maybe she didn't have the gift of time with her children, but she had the love for them in her heart. That was a blessing and an answer to her final prayer. In my heart and hers, she was a mother.

●

My parents are hurting just looking at me; I can see it in their eyes. Their pain is different. They did not lose a child, though they loved Ronnie dearly. They are suffering, watching their son in pain. They are frustrated and feeling helpless, like everyone else, knowing that there is nothing they can do.

Mom hugged me tightly this morning and said, "I wish I could trade places with her."

I understood her words because I would have done the same thing in a second.

●

Calling Ronnie's memorial a "celebration of life" made it sound like a joyful event—which was perhaps fitting because hers was indeed a joyful life. So many people loved her and so many will miss her; it was a happy kind of sad.

More than three thousand red roses, Ronnie's favorite flower, lined the altar, and their scent permeated every corner of the church. They created a warm and familiar feeling, as if we were at home, in her garden.

In Ronnie's eulogy, I made a public and very personal commitment to life, to family, and to love. I think God has a plan for each and every one of us. Ronnie was a teacher not only to me but to all whose lives she touched.

One thing I've already learned is this: Life is fragile. Not just mine but the lives of those all around me. Every breath we take is a precious gift. We need to remember to love, and to cherish, and to help others *now*—not at some vague time in the future.

Cards and letters keep pouring in from friends and family all over the world. I open them all, and day after day I read them and cry. Ronnie was greatly loved, and although I knew this when she was alive, the steady flood of love coming in every day comforts me.

I recently received a long letter from a close friend who had been with me when I fell in love with Ronnie on a trip to the Grand Canyon. Barry and Ronnie had the same sense of humor, and they knew each other quite well. Like the rest of us, he was struggling to understand.

He began, "It took one of the most special people we have ever met to penetrate the armor of our daily clutter in which we've cocooned ourselves. Work, money, cars, houses, shopping for dinner, laundry, bills. Why does it take a tragedy to lift the shades and illuminate the important things in life?

"I do not pretend to understand why this happened, but my gut tells me that the good will uncover itself in time. This is the only good reason I can think of and perhaps this is Ronnie's legacy. Her life and death will permanently alter many lives for the better.

"If the death of someone can fan away the fog and improve even one person's life, then maybe that's a gift. I believe Ronnie is delivering presents even now to many, many people."

I stopped reading for a moment and looked out to her garden. Red roses were blooming everywhere, more gorgeous and perfect presents from Ronnie. Barry's next words surprised me.

"Mark, right now you are the unluckiest person in the world. You are also one of the luckiest. Most people go through life with one, two, or maybe a small handful of people that get invited across the bridge into the 'good friends' camp. People who truly care about you, think often about you, never question you, share your complete honesty, listen to you, and will be there to support and help you when tragedy hits. Some campsites are barren wastelands with one sad person sitting by a smoldering fire.

"You may not see it yet, but you are incredibly blessed. The outpouring of love and support has been for Ronnie, but it is for you, too. I have rediscovered through this that the distinction between good friends and family is blurred. I believe with absolute certainty that you will be happy again one day.

"Your campsite is a crowded bonfire with lots of good friends. I like to think it's on the Grand Canyon where we all became friends, and Ronnie is out there, somewhere, with us.

"Somehow, inconceivably, the world is a little better place today. And I feel a little bit wiser. My gift from Ronnie Lew."

That was a beautiful message of hope for me, but the future seems like such a faraway place. I hope his insight proves to be right.

It seems a lifetime since she was near me. Alone at night, I stare at her picture. I find myself clutching her favorite pillow and I've drifted over to her side of the bed. Each night is lonelier than the last, yet the mornings are the most difficult. It's hard to face another day without her.

I still can't believe she's gone. I can close my eyes and still feel the warmth of her breath, the parting of her lips, the weight of her chest resting on mine. Her every curve and scent and pleasure seemed to be made just for me. And they were—just as she was—made just for me.

But I wonder now: Was my life and love equally well-suited and designed for her? Would she close her eternal eyes and remember us as we once were? Or would she recall me as cold and distant from all the work and ambition that at times had dominated my waking moments?

It's not just the long hours I spent working into the night. It was the ease with which I left her behind. Yet she seemed so proud to be my wife. If only there had been more time. We were supposed to grow old together.

(M)

They say that you can't take it with you, but they were wrong. All that I had is gone. Ronnie has taken it all with her. It's ironic that I am content in knowing she will never have to feel this pain. She will never be left behind.

I have this disturbing vision that keeps me awake at night. A little boy sits strapped in an empty shopping cart in the middle of a busy grocery store. He cannot find his mother and becomes frightened. People are busy all around him. They don't really notice him. He is lost and alone, waiting for her to return. That is how I feel.

I keep seeing women who remind me of Ronnie. Maybe it's someone with a similar hairstyle or who walks like she did. For a second I will have this impulse to run up to that person. I know it isn't really her, but I still have to fight the urge to hope for the impossible. And then she turns to look at me or I hear her speak, and I know it is someone else's wife or lover or friend.

Sometimes I must stop and wonder why. It seems so unfair and senseless. Why did God allow this? Why must I lose the only thing of any real value in my life?

These are good questions with no good answers. I feel such deep sadness. I often wish I could have been there to make her feel unafraid and to welcome her into heaven with open arms—though I'm sure God was there instead.

Time is not the healer, but clearly, healing takes time. At the moment, I feel like half a man living half a life. So many of the best parts of me came from her. Was it really that wonderful or am I just remembering it that way? I know life wasn't perfect, but it seemed so close.

I'm beginning to see two lives going on inside of me. One life is trying to remember the past, trying to keep everything just the way it was. At first I couldn't even move a chair without thinking about the change it created. The other life knows that my memories of Ronnie will always keep her alive in my spirit. She would want me to move on and to start a new life.

At times God reminds me how fortunate I am to have had so much to lose. My heart continues to ache, yet hope fills my empty future.

SELF-PITY IS QUITE IMMOBILIZING, NOT to mention extremely unattractive. It's clear I need a wake-up call, a reason to stop feeling sorry for myself. My plans have taken a dramatic turn toward the unknown, and I'm facing an uncertain future as a single, pregnant, first-time mother-to-be. But what is the big deal? I've handled stress and instability before. I'm independent and have never really needed anyone to rescue me. Maybe my life hasn't been easy, but I've always managed to make it on my own.

So, why am I sitting all alone at the kitchen counter with my weary head in my hands, feeling sorry for myself? How long can I waste energy questioning myself, wondering, "What was I thinking? How could I have let this happen?"

It's amazing how perspective can change in one moment. Yesterday, in the midst of my wallowing, my friend Dave called me. I hadn't heard from him in months, and I imagined that he was calling to sympathize with my unfortunate situation, but that wasn't to be the case at all.

"Have you heard about Mark's wife?" he asked.

I remembered Dave bringing Mark and his wife, Ronnie, to my restaurant a few times. They were always lovingly holding hands, while I was hustling and bustling through my days. Once I saw them in a shopping mall; they were strolling along together, again holding hands. I was in a rush to buy panty hose or something equally ridiculous, and I passed by them. I barely stopped to say hello, but that was how I was, always on a mission. That was the last time I had seen them, but I had heard she was finally pregnant.

"No, why?" I wondered.

There was pain in his voice. "She died on Mother's Day. The triplets died, too."

I was stunned. "That's unbelievable," I said, before all the obvious questions about the specifics. I wondered to myself why details are so often a prerequisite for grasping a situation, especially a tragedy.

Dave went on, "Mark is absolutely devastated. All he does is walk around the house and the garden looking for pieces of what he calls his past life. He doesn't even want anyone to do the laundry. He asks everyone not to touch or move anything. Nothing can change. I think he needs to get out of the house."

It turned out that Dave was calling not just to tell me what had happened to Ronnie but to encourage me to have lunch with him and Mark sometime the following week. I wondered why he had called me. What could I possibly have to say to a man whose wife had just died? I nervously and reluctantly said yes. What else could I say to Dave? He's such a close friend, and I knew he wouldn't have asked unless it was important to him.

I hung up the phone. My problems instantly became insignificant compared with Mark's.

A moment before Dave's call I had been thinking my life was somehow a failure, but in truth I was fortunate and suddenly also thankful. There was a precious treasure growing inside me, a child to hold and love. My life was moving forward while Mark's had come to a screeching halt.

It's only lunch, so why do I feel compelled to call my girlfriends to help me decide what to wear? We all agree that the real issue is my protruding belly. It needs to be hidden; that's my priority. My pregnancy is not a secret to Mark or anyone else, but I don't want my bulging waistline to be a reminder of his loss.

D

Coping with tragedy is not my strength. Add to that a dose of initial shyness and there I was, at a local café with Mark and Dave, feeling out of place and speechless.

It was hard not to talk about Ronnie; it was so soon after her death, and Mark was visibly sad. I really didn't know what to say. A mention of travel would provoke a memory of a past vacation. Talk of the future was uncomfortable. There was an awkward understanding that Mark's future was no longer the beautiful dream he held in his heart with his wife and three children.

At first, I couldn't wait for lunch to be over so my tension could dissolve and I could go home, but by the time we were drinking coffee and relaxing a bit, something had changed. I realized that Mark was comfortable being sad. How could he be any other way? It made sense; his heart was hurting. Once Dave and I became comfortable with Mark's sadness, we enjoyed our time together. Soon I was feeling like I was in the presence of two good friends.

After lunch, Dave and I went back to his office. "Thanks for taking the time to get together with us. I hope it wasn't too uncomfortable for you," he said.

"No, not at all. It was my pleasure, but I don't think I was very helpful. He seems like he's going to be sad for a long, long time," I answered.

"Yeah, he's in a lot of pain. He says he feels like he's been ripped in half," Dave explained.

"He looks like it," I said. "You can see it in his distant eyes and even in his lonely hands. He was fidgeting constantly, like he was looking for something to hold."

Dave looked right at me. "Personally, I think Mark is one of those people who may never get married again. It's going to be hard for him to move on. He loved Ronnie so much I doubt he will ever find someone else to love as much."

I stared back at him, and the words seemed to come not from my mouth but from my heart. I said, "You know what, Dave? I think he will marry again for that very reason. A man with the capacity to love a woman that deeply will surely fall in love again."

D

The three of us had dinner together last Friday in an Italian restaurant with bright fluorescent lights and no ambiance. The atmosphere was fitting, almost as if the mood was determined for us before we arrived. The sterile walls were shouting at us, telling us loud and clear that intimacy was not an option.

After dinner Mark and I exchanged e-mail addresses and agreed to keep in touch. I let Mark know that I was still a bit of a dinosaur in the area of technology, but I promised to send him e-mail. I arrived home after dinner and turned on my computer. I seemed to have no trouble navigating my way to the right place, though I wasn't absolutely sure how to send a letter.

I typed, "Did I find you?" and sent it away.

Within two minutes I got a simple reply: "Yes, you found me."

I couldn't help myself. I went to bed that night with Mark on my mind.

SUMMER

Dave doesn't chaperone us anymore. Walks along the beach and long coastal drives have become regular activities for us. We talk for hours at a time. From the very first time we met for lunch alone, we've been comfortable with each other. Somehow it's easy for Mark to cry with me. I'm not there to fix him, change him, or heal him. I know I'm not capable of any of that, so I'm simply there.

He's told me about the rafting trip on the Grand Canyon when he met Ronnie. He's told stories about all their travel adventures to Greece, Tonga, Sumatra, Italy, Austria, and the last winter they spent together in Lake Tahoe. I've learned all about creating Koosh toys from rubber bands and the ingenious contraption his brother-in-law invented to make them.

Every day at 3:05 P.M., Mark's wristwatch alarm sounds as a reminder of the time of day when Ronnie died.

Our friends have been cautioning us constantly not to spend so much time together, and we understand why.

They are worried about us. Is Mark on the rebound? Are we each looking for an easy replacement for the love and family we long for? We've talked rationally about everyone's valid concerns and have decided that, even if this time together is just for healing and friendship, we are a gift in each other's lives. We're aware that we are both at the most vulnerable point in our lives, but we just can't stop.

And as my belly grows, so does our attraction to each other.

Mark surprised me after dinner the other evening by leaning over and kissing me. It wasn't a long or particularly passionate kiss, but it was a tender moment. I had been secretly hoping for that kiss for a while.

I've learned a lot about Ronnie—that she was nearly flawless, in fact, perfect, at least as memorialized in Mark's mind. Their life together was like a beautiful waltz until the day the music stopped playing. Mark loved her, and everyone else did, too. That's a tough act to follow, especially for me.

In my entire life I have never known anyone who was perfect. In fact, I have gravitated toward the imperfect among us. Most of my close friends have had difficulties in life and have struggled many years to discover themselves. There is a certain camaraderie among "us." The people we have become today are each like the phoenix rising from the ashes, emerging strong and confident.

So, here we are, Mark and I together, and I am not Ronnie. I'm beginning to see how that is often difficult for Mark to accept. Sometimes I frustrate him, and I can see why. Everything between us happened so suddenly. He wants his old life back, and that is the one thing that I can never give him.

I am not living under the illusion that our relationship, or any relationship, should or even could ever be perfect. I take these roadblocks as opportunities for growth and deeper understanding. Usually, in the beginning of a relationship the problems are clouded by the bliss. But I haven't gotten that with Mark. We skipped the bliss and dove right into each other's problems. There's the normal stuff and a whole lot more.

We've both been wondering if our friends who say we are moving too fast are actually right. We are falling in love with each other. We want to know everything about each other and we're impatient. We justify our haste by acknowledging that neither of us is often prone to poor judgment in regard to people. Still I have to question, is this really right or do we just want it to be? I know some serious bumps are still lying in the road ahead.

Some of my friends are taking a quick trip to Mexico in a couple of weeks. I'm more in the mood to stay home and nest, but maybe a week away is a good idea right now.

I was right. It was good to have some time to think. The dry, desert heat made sleeping difficult, and so in the middle of the first night I found myself on a lounge chair near the pool, looking up at the sky. The moon was full and never more beautiful than it was that night. It was so peaceful. I rubbed my pregnant belly and felt a deep love for the baby girl growing inside me.

One of my dearest and funniest friends—known by her nickname, Smedgie—came out and joined me. We both had insomnia, but for different reasons. Mine was due to pregnancy, hers due to menopause. Beginnings and endings, we were at different places in the cycle of life.

At about three o'clock in the morning we decided to take a swim in the pool. The water was warm and calming. We talked until the sun came up about our lives, our fears and self-doubts. We talked about Mark and the concerns I was having.

"Sometimes I feel like I'm just not good enough for him," I explained. "I feel like he judges me, or compares me, which makes me insecure. Then I wonder, how can I compete with his perfect family, perfect wife, perfect life?"

"Don't worry, Diane. He just doesn't know you like we do yet." Smedgie gave me a big hug.

"I know. It's just that I've spent a lot of years getting to a point where I feel good about myself and now I'm with a guy who wants me to be someone else."

"Are you in love with him?" Smedgie asked me.

"I think so, but I'm just not sure I know him," I answered.

She looked puzzled, so I went on, "Maybe under less complicated circumstances it would be obvious. I know he cares about me, but he is still so in love with someone else. And he is often so sad and distant. I understand completely, but I don't know if his distance is really who he is or just a temporary result of his circumstances."

I was scared and she knew it.

The next day we swam for hours in the Sea of Cortez. I was weightless in the water, which was so relaxing. That night we had a fabulous Mexican fiesta at the Trailer Park Café, and though we laughed and enjoyed ourselves, at times I silently wished Mark was with us. Later, Smedgie and I found ourselves swimming in the pool again in the middle of the night.

I knew I was in for a lecture. Smedgie began, "You know, Diane, you need to take care of yourself and your baby right now. Maybe the timing just isn't right with Mark and you'd be better off alone."

"So I'm supposed to just stop caring for him? Just like that?" I became defensive.

"He's a great guy, Diane, but he's got so much baggage. A dead perfect wife is a lot of baggage."

I couldn't control myself even though I knew she was right, "Baggage? You want to talk about baggage? Look at me. I'm the one with the baggage. I'm emotional, opinionated, stubborn, and to top it off, I'm unemployed and pregnant."

"You're right, Diane. You're a project, too."

After thinking about it for several minutes, she added, "I've spent my entire life looking for someone over the age of five with no baggage and I haven't found one person yet. At least with Mark you know he doesn't have commitment problems."

"So what do I do?" I asked her.

"Embrace the baggage," she said, smiling.

IT'S BEEN A SCORCHING CALIFORNIA summer. Since Diane came back from Mexico, we've spent a lot of time by the pool at her condo. One day last week, Diane was in the pool floating, which she now calls her favorite sport. I had some magazines to read, and she had brought a book filled with over ten thousand baby names. I picked it up and flipped through.

Diane swam over to the edge, and I asked her, "Have you thought of any new names for the baby yet?"

"No," she replied, "If it were a boy, it would be easy. I'd name him Charlie, after my grandfather. I suppose she could be Rosemary, after my mom and grandmother, but that just sounds so old-fashioned."

As she swam away she called out to me, "Why don't you take a look? Maybe you can find a name."

Always up for a challenge, I opened the book and started reading.

Diane's grandfather had been a kind and generous doctor, but what Diane admired most about him was his humility and his sense of humor. His humor apparently saved them from many tears. He had loved mint jelly. He would eat it with anything. During the last week of his life, at a rather solemn moment he said to his family, "You know, I'm really going to miss mint jelly."

When he died, Diane was holding him in her arms. She said that the windows were open and there was a cool breeze blowing in his bedroom. His eyes closed and there was a big smile on his face. He knew he was going to heaven. At the same moment the church bells rang and echoed a sweet melody in the room. He had lived in peace and died in peace. I prayed it had been like that for Ronnie.

I knew it would mean a lot to Diane if she could honor him, so I looked up the name Charles, which led me through a list of boy's names and eventually to a section of girl's names. I looked over the list until I read one that sounded just right. The name was Carly.

I looked up the name Rosemary. Directly following it was the abbreviated version, Rose.

"I got it," I said to Diane after only about five minutes.

"Already?"

"Carly Rose," I said.

She smiled at me and said, "I love it. Carly Rose. It's perfect."

I am learning to accept that my life will never return to the life I left behind the day Ronnie died. Even the simple things have changed forever. My clothes will never be folded the same way and my routines will probably never be the way I remember they used to be each and every morning. Everything is different.

Though sometimes I seem to regress and take a step back in time, it has become obvious that I am looking and hoping for a heart that no longer beats. Ronnie and I will not grow old together. I know I cannot go back. There is nothing there but loneliness. So where do I go from here? It's time to move forward.

I must be healing, at least a little, because lately my days have been filled with anticipation rather than wishful uncertainty. I may even be getting excited about the future, but it's still so confusing. I'm becoming more accustomed to my loss, more resigned to my "fate." Certainty is a thing of the past. I am beginning to have a glimmer of hope and curiosity about the future.

I can't quite explain the feeling I had last night. Diane and I went out for dinner. It was so strange sitting across the table from another woman and looking into her eyes. Somehow, as if I had an epiphany, it occurred to me that they weren't Ronnie's dark eyes I was gazing into. They were blue. They were beautiful yet so unfamiliar.

The restaurant was familiar, but in so many ways the woman was still a stranger to me. And I was even a bit of a stranger to myself, editing my words and concerned with my table manners as if I was going to leave with a report card. Etiquette has never been a concern of mine, and I am not used to being so self-conscious. It's been a long time since I worried about what someone else thought about me. Not that I didn't have a good time. Diane was pleasant, funny, and also seemed to enjoy herself.

And so did I. She is so understanding, but I can see that getting used to someone new will be a slow process for me. My habits are just so ingrained. I hope she can be patient with me; I hope her grandfather taught her that, too.

Circumstances change, life changes, and of that we can be certain. We often hear that nothing good lasts forever—that is the bad news. But we also need to remember the inverse: nothing bad lasts forever, either.

Diane is beginning to feel comfortable around my house. When she is here, it feels like a home again. She enjoys her quiet days with me and seems content with simplicity. I want to feel that contentment again myself. Today I watched Diane outside the back window. She was leaning over in Ronnie's garden, smelling each rose, as if each one had its own unique scent.

She has been supportive and a source of great comfort for me, yet I fear I hurt her often with my distance and poorly chosen words. Words are powerful tools, but they can also be potent weapons. I must learn to choose more wisely. A heart is a tender thing, and I should know that better than most.

I have so much to learn. Maybe the formative years never really end.

I'm also beginning to believe that maybe one thing does last forever—love.

M

I've changed. My confidence is shaken and I no longer trust my intuition. It is difficult to recognize my old self sometimes because I still choose to live in fear. It may, understandably, be the fear of loving again, but on a deeper level it may really be the fear of losing again. No one would ever want to endure such heartache twice in one lifetime. Nevertheless, I finally get it: I am responsible for my own happiness, and this fear is a ball and chain around my ankles.

It is time to let go of the past, embrace the present moment, and peacefully look forward to tomorrow. Diane fills my heart and brings me joy again. She deserves to have all of me. I must cease the relentless excuses and make a choice to live a full life right now. Simply existing is not an option. I cannot give up on life or life will surely give up on me. There are still dreams left to fill, and I know Ronnie would want that for me.

It is time.

Earlier today, I was sitting at the dining-room table and looking out to the garden. Diane's back was toward me and she was kneeling down. She was wearing a soft green floral dress with a plain white T-shirt underneath. For a moment I saw Ronnie. My thoughts flashed back to the way she looked in her favorite dress, the one I later buried her in.

I felt sad, but as Diane stood and turned toward me, I was filled with something deeper. I realized at that moment that time was indeed healing. At first, perhaps, Diane was filling a gap in my life. But over time, our love has grown into much more than a replacement for the love I lost. She is special and different. Together we are different. And even though my love for Ronnie is still here, I feel free to love again.

New seeds have been planted and new flowers are ready to bloom.

PART ONE

DIANE

THE MOVEMENT IN MY STOMACH HAS been an unusual source of entertainment for us lately. We could charge admission because it's been quite a show. Mark sings songs and plays the guitar, usually either James Taylor or the Beatles. I sit close to him, and within less than a minute Carly will start dancing in my stomach—arms and legs flying around. Every once in a while we are convinced she knows the Macarena.

With the exception of the usual complaints, my pregnancy was pure joy. Up until the day before Carly was born I went to the gym. I took the trip to Mexico with my friends and spent lots of time with Mark. All that freedom and fun was intertwined with lots of emotions and difficulty, but I generally stayed healthy and happy in spite of the unusual circumstances. Life has certainly changed in these past few months.

To my surprise, birth was also pure joy. Seeing Carly's little body and holding her in my arms for the first time was absolutely the most beautiful and present moment of my life. I know that Mark loved her the moment he saw her, too.

It was difficult knowing that Ronnie had died right down the hall from where I had just experienced the incomparable miracle of birth. Life and death were separated only by a cold corridor of unopened doors. And if it bothered me, I know it must have been so much harder for Mark, the bittersweet blending of old memories and new. I am reminded of life's unpredictability, and that spontaneity is not a positive word where death is concerned.

Within hours after Carly was born, I was inspired to write a letter for her to read someday. Memories may fade, but they are also the building blocks of history. Experiences are the bricks, but our feelings are the mortar that holds a relationship together forever. Carly will hear the story of her birth a dozen times, but I also want her to know my feelings.

Mark cradled Carly in his arms and sang to her as I began to write. I have since addressed this letter, sealed it, and mailed it to Carly. On the back I printed, "To open when your first child is born."

To open when your first child is born

Dear Carly,

Can you believe it? No one could ever imagine what birth is like until they've experienced it firsthand. Never has anything taken over my life with such power. I felt so scared and so confident at the same time. Most of all, I just wanted to see you, know that you were healthy, and hold you in my arms. The doctors said to rest up so I would have plenty of energy for delivery, but I couldn't sleep. I stayed awake all night wondering what you would look like and praying you would be healthy.

I went to the hospital and began what turned out to be the most unbelievably painful experience of my life. As my contractions became more severe, I remember thinking, "This is probably as bad as pain can get. I can take it." And then the pain would intensify, and I couldn't believe that something this beautiful could hurt this much.

What a miracle! You were born at 9:27 P.M. on October 18, 1996. You weighed eight pounds and three ounces. You are a beautiful girl. I will never forget this day and the moment I first held you in my arms.

The sweetest, most beautiful bundle of love is sleeping soundly in the crib next to me. God is amazing. I can't stop crying, just looking at you. Sometimes I feel like I don't know what to do, but Mother Nature is an incredible guide.

I have heard that, as the years go by, of all the experiences in life, birth and child-raising will keep you in the present moment more than anything else. This is a gift in itself. I can feel that already. My perspective on life has changed in an instant.

Just the idea of you hurting in your lifetime for any reason saddens me so. Everyone knows that life includes a certain amount of sorrow and pain. But I look at you now, so innocent and pure. If I could wrap you in my arms and protect you for a lifetime I would, but that is not life. What I can do is give you guidance, showing you how to weather life's challenges with grace and how to be grateful for God's abundant love. Remember I will always be here for you.

> *You are deeply loved,*
> *Mom*

To Mark, this baby is the earthly equivalent of an angel. We are all so fortunate. Months ago we were worried about the day Carly would arrive and how that would change us. We were so excited, yet we wondered if this would be the time that our paths would separate, that our needs would collide, and if the magnitude of our circumstances would cause us to walk away from each other. To my relief and happiness, we grew even closer.

I'm convinced that Mark is made of Velcro. Carly is always stuck somewhere on him. Her first naps were spent snuggled into Mark's chest.

Healing is a long process, maybe even a lifelong one. I understand that there are actually two lives going on inside of Mark's heart. He is holding on to an old love while falling in love with Carly and me. It is so simple yet so complex. It is one of those times when absolute acceptance is critical. I have to let him go through it, all of it. I have been told repeatedly about the "one-year grief cycle"—and have recently been accused of interrupting the "process." Maybe it's true, but love is not like a waterspout that I can just turn off.

One cold and dreary day we were driving in the pouring rain to a doctor's appointment. Along the roadside there were giant puddles, and it sounded like thousands of tiny needles were dropping on the roof of our car.

At the stoplight, Mark looked over at me and said, "People are worried because I'm starting to live again. Are you?"

His question took me by surprise. I answered him cautiously, "If anything, I'm concerned that sometimes I get in the way of your sadness. People say you need time to heal. The doctors told you that most people need a year, and if you feel that way too, I want you to have that time."

He pulled over to the side of the road and parked. "Diane, I have cried with you almost every day for months now. I am grieving, I am sad, but what are my options? Do I help others to grieve as well by sitting alone in my house waiting for visitors to stop by to share their tears with me? Or do I take the lesson we all learned from Ronnie's death, to live each moment as the special gift that it is?"

"I know, it must be confusing for you," I reassured him. It was confusing for me, too.

Mark continued, "They don't realize that I will continue to grieve, maybe forever. Even the doctor tells me I should be angry, but there is no one to blame. Who would I get angry at? God? Why should I blame God for giving me so much, for filling me so full?"

I nodded in understanding and wondered silently where he was going with his thoughts. It was a common feeling I had. One thing I learned about Mark was that he appreciated someone who could sit with him and just listen. He is the type who can be comforted by silence.

Staring out at Marin General Hospital, Mark said, "Not long ago I followed a screeching ambulance carrying my wife and three unborn children to the front door of that building. It was dark and rainy, just like today. That is where they died, the final destination in their journey on earth."

His eyes were watering as he continued, "A few weeks ago I arrived back at that same building. It was a crisp and bright fall day. I hugged you, put Carly safely in her car seat, and drove the two of you home. That is where she was born, the first destination in her journey here on earth."

"A lot has changed so quickly, hasn't it?" I started to understand.

Mark continued, "And how can I possibly make sense of this? Both events were life-changing. Both remind me that life is precious. But we each grieve differently and in our own time, and to spend my days wondering why these things happen is like placing a limit on God's love for me. God's ways are not our ways, and I may never know why Ronnie died."

Not knowing what to say, I offered him my hand.

"Well, we can either move forward cautiously or wait for social convention to give us permission. A lot has happened, but we're here together now and I love you."

He started the car and we drove away.

I recently realized that the letter I wrote to Carly in the hospital was only one of many times I would want to preserve memories for her. Mark was inspired by my idea; now he plans to write her letters as well. In our desire to communicate our love to Carly throughout her life, our plans have become more elaborate. We have bought a journal of sorts and made it into what we call the "Letter Box." Although I couldn't resist decorating it, the exterior is not the point. It's simple, but as the years go by we intend to fill it to overflowing with love, memories, and dreams.

I've written a letter to explain the gift to Carly. It will remain sealed until the day she receives it, which will likely be her high school graduation day.

All the other letters we will write for the different seasons she will experience in her lifetime will be sealed and mailed to our home. The cancelled postage on the outside will make each envelope a mini–time capsule, with a stamp and date that freezes the letter in a moment of history. We will keep them in the Letter Box. The letters will be for good times and bad, but each and every one will contain the pure essence of our love for her. What a joy it will be to share this with her throughout the experiences in our lives!

Dear Carly,

Today you are so young and curious. I want to remember everything from the first time I heard you cry till the day you leave for college, but I know that I will not remember it all, so I am attempting to preserve some history for you now, while the memories are still fresh in my mind.

This Letter Box is a lifelong gift to you. I wrote you the first letter a few hours after you were born. That one, and all the others, have been written for you to open on a special milestone in your life. Please open each letter on that day.

I am inspired to create this gift because I often wonder where the years will take us. What adventures and hardships will we share? How will you live your life? My hope is that you are filled with confidence and love that you find peace and take joy in the simplest pleasures. I pray that you laugh often and ride with dignity and grace down life's sometimes bumpy roads.

Maybe when you open some of these letters, I will be sitting by your side so I can tell you stories and laugh with you. Perhaps you will live far away and we will talk on the telephone. But if God has taken me from this earth, let this book be a living legacy of my love and pride for you.

You are the greatest joy I have ever known, and I don't want to miss a single reason to celebrate your life, even if only in spirit.

> *I will love you through all the years,*
> *Mom*

PILES OF BOOKS HAVE STACKED UP IN the corner of the room, all unopened, all thoughtful gifts received over these past months from well-meaning friends and relatives. I started off in a deep, dark place with very little interest in crawling out. Few knew what to say, but everyone wanted to help. My world had been turned upside down and shaken, and various continents had fallen off. God's spirit was with me, but my spirit, I felt, had left.

And then along came Diane. She was somehow easy—a comforting, accepting place to rest. She took my mind off starting over and allowed me to be sad and uncertain. I never felt pressure.

Out of chaos and turmoil she has gradually found my remaining pieces and polished them until they shine. She found enough of me to make a new person again, although I can only imagine that it was quite a large project to undertake. I know with certainty that she didn't take this project on by chance but by providence.

Now I realize that Diane and Carly have been placed in my life for much more than just putting me back together again. There is joy, and hope, and a life to plan and care for.

As I contemplate a life with Diane, a friend of mine has said to me, "Are you crazy? You could be one of the most eligible bachelors in town."

I responded without hesitation, "I'd prefer to be one of the most happily married men instead."

Earlier today, Diane created another memory for Carly's letter box. It is a true story, written for Carly, but a very special memory for Diane. I'm beginning to understand the power of the letter box. It will someday be a priceless treasure for Carly, but it is also a key that opens the door to Diane's heart. Those letters hold her deepest thoughts and say so much about how she feels.

When she finished writing the letter she came upstairs, handed it to me, and said, "I wrote this for Carly's letter box, but it is also for you."

Inside the envelope were two pieces of light blue stationery trimmed with colorful fish and a photo of an old man I had never seen before.

Dear Carly,

It was 4:30 A.M. on a crisp, foggy San Francisco morning. The salmon-fishing boat had left the pier in Sausalito. We were headed out for a day trip out of the bay and under the Golden Gate Bridge. I was the only woman, surrounded by eighteen salty old men of the sea. I never would have guessed that this would be the day I learned what true love really means, but it was.

As the sun rose and the boat pounded through the waves, I spotted an old man with a sweet face sitting on a bench. He was looking at some photographs. Nausea was setting in and I needed to sit down, so I asked if I could join him.

Henry was from Los Angeles. He was 96 and had just driven himself up to Sausalito the night before to go on this fishing trip. He showed me the photos of himself and his wife. The photo was old, but it looked like they were on the exact same boat we were on that day. They were fishing together.

Apparently they would drive up to Sausalito once every year for a day of fishing. Then they would put the catch in a cooler, head back to Los Angeles, and have a huge party and salmon barbecue with all of their friends.

He said his wife loved to fish more than he did, and I wondered why he had come alone. Soon he told me that his wife had died earlier that year and one of the last things she told him was to keep on fishing. And so he did.

He cried as he talked of their love and the memories of their life together. This was before I had met your dad, so I had never experienced such love or such loss. I couldn't even imagine the pain he was experiencing. I must confess I selfishly wondered about myself as he spoke. Would I ever know a love like that? Would a man ever miss me so much that he would feel as if his body had been ripped in half when I was gone?

I made a commitment to myself that day on that dirty, smelly boat to make love a priority in my life. No longer would I wait for Mr. Perfect. After all, I certainly wasn't Ms. Perfect. No longer would I be too busy for love.

During the same time I was taking a photography class at the Academy of Art College in San Francisco, and my assignment was to take some pictures in the fog. I had my camera and snapped two full rolls of the old man reeling in what would most likely be the last salmon of his lifetime. He was smiling, and he began to relax and enjoy the day. We talked, and I cried with him, and then we fished some more. Thank God the fish were biting.

After the final exam in my photography class, I packed up the photos of Henry and sent them to him in Los Angeles. I knew he would love them. His spirit was shining in every shot; clearly, he believed his wife was there with him.

Several weeks later I received a letter in the mail. It was from his daughter. She was writing to thank me for the photos. He had told her all about his trip and his day of fishing on the bay, but he never got to see the photos. She said that her father had passed away and these were the last photos ever taken of him. She was so pleased he was smiling. The pictures had confirmed what she had always known about her parents: Love was the foundation of their world.

That day taught me what really matters in life. When you find true love, the pieces of the puzzle will fit together and you will feel safe and secure. True love lives on and on for-

ever. I know that now. I have that love in my heart, and I
pray for a love like that for you. Keep your heart wide open.

Love,
Mom

Diane has added so much to my life. In fact, she has given a life back to me, the very life I thought I had lost forever. She is so generous with her heart, and I imagine that is exactly how she'll still be fifty years from now.

Maybe that's why, when I looked in the mirror this morning, I saw the face of a man who may be ready for marriage. It startled me at first because I hadn't welcomed that thought before, but I am fortunate to have found a gentle woman who honors my past and the other woman I loved so dearly. God has blessed me with a loving companion and also with a beautiful child.

We headed off to Hawaii for a vacation on the North Shore, with Carly asleep in my arms. The airline celebrated its anniversary that day, complete with games and prizes and an overall mood of relaxation and fun.

The flight attendant came by with a large dessert tray. Though Diane declined, after the attendant had served me my dessert, she put a small box on a dessert plate on Diane's tray. "And this one is for you," she said to Diane, smiling. "Enjoy your dessert."

Diane leaned over to me and said, "Why is everyone always giving me chocolate?"

She kept talking with me about Hawaii, asking me so many questions because she knew I wanted to live there. Finally, I looked over at her tray and said, "Open the box. Let's see what's in it."

Diane handed me the box and said, "You can open it. The last thing I need is more chocolate. You're the skinny one."

I gave her what she describes as "the look," and she reluctantly said, "OK, I'll open it, but don't let me eat any."

She opened the box. Inside was a small black velvet box. "Maybe it's earplugs," I joked.

"Or really good chocolate," she said. She smiled and looked at me. She opened the velvet box, and tears filled her eyes as she pulled out a plain and simple platinum wedding band, the one she once said she had always wanted.

I proposed to her on the plane, and by the time we landed on Oahu we had decided to get married in California as soon as we could plan our wedding. There was every reason to wait, but we didn't want to.

DIANE

OUR GRAND WEDDING PLANS SOON became complicated and increasingly difficult to coordinate. Our goal was to keep our life as simple as possible—just like the wedding band—and this was no way to get started.

One morning last week, as we were having coffee on the porch watching the waves, I said to Mark, "Who are those people with the patience and enthusiasm to plan a year in advance for a wedding? Not me, that's for sure. I know my mom wishes I wanted to plan an elaborate and formal wedding, but I just don't want to take the time."

"Well, then how do you feel?" he asked.

"I just don't want to become frustrated and stressed planning the most special day of our life together," I explained.

"Hmmm," he muttered under his breath, and I looked at him wondering what exactly that meant.

We sat quietly for a minute. I could tell Mark was thinking. His eyes were gazing far away, beyond the horizon. This particular look usually means that something profound or at least thought-provoking was about to come out of his mouth.

He turned to me and asked, "Can your mom get here in the next three days?"

"I think so. Why?" I wondered.

"Let's get married here. I mean right here on this beach," he said.

"In three days?"

"I'd marry you in three minutes if I could. Let's do it in three days." Mark's enthusiasm and determination is very convincing. I listened, trying to weigh his points against the fact that I'd waited so many years for the day I'd be joining my life with a man I knew I would love forever. Sensing my openness to the idea, he continued, "Why wait? We've got plenty of experiences and challenges ahead of us, and I'd like to start facing all of them as a family."

Mark's choice of the words "as a family" proved more convincing than any comments that followed.

We changed our grand plans and opted instead for a small but intimate ceremony on the beach in the backyard. Within a couple of hours, we arranged for our mothers and my aunt to fly over, and we invited a couple of neighborhood friends. We ordered leis and a cake and even arranged for a photographer to come.

That same morning, I ventured out alone to the next town, Haleiwa, and went to Silver Moon, a fashionable women's clothing store. I knew what I wanted. A white dress, not a wedding gown, just a simple white dress I could wear without shoes on the beach.

Within twenty minutes I had picked out my wedding dress. I surprised Mark when I returned home before noon.

We found a bright floral dress for Carly and a Hawaiian aloha shirt for Mark. Before we knew it, the wedding was planned and we were on our way to the airport to pick up our guests.

Three days after Mark suggested the idea, the wedding took place. Our local Hawaiian minister performed much of it in Hawaiian. Even though we definitely did say "I do," I still wonder sometimes if we are officially married. I have no idea what I agreed to. I just said yes to everything. Mark claims that was to his advantage.

Who needs a honeymoon when you get married in Hawaii? I was so happy to wake up the next morning with Mark and watch the sun come up and listen to the waves crashing along the shore.

Later that morning, Carly was sleeping soundly by my side and Mark was out surfing. I could see him in the distance. There were several surfers out at the surf break that day, but I could tell which one was Mark. They all begin to have a signature style that sets them apart from the others. I recognize Mark by his wobbly arms. He may not like that, but it's true.

It was a peaceful time, so I decided to add to Carly's letter box while the memories of our wedding day were still dancing in my mind.

Dear Carly,

Yesterday was a day that you will never remember but I will never forget. Today I am sitting here looking at you, a tiny angel, and imagining the day many years from now when you will walk down the aisle and into the arms of your husband.

I wonder what music you will dance to on your wedding day. I wonder if you are young or a late bloomer like your mom. I could never make up my mind because I always wanted to wait for Mr. Perfect. So I waited and waited and waited. And then finally I met your dad.

It's clear I have married someone very different from me. He knew what he wanted early in life. He was always such a committed man. I respected that about him from the moment I met him.

On our wedding day I woke up grinning from ear to ear. It was before dawn and even the birds were still sleeping. I just sat on the porch and waited patiently for the sun to rise.

For a long time I pondered my future. I imagined how my family would grow, becoming part of his family. I imagined how our friendships would grow and merge and change over the years. I wondered how many children we would have.

And then suddenly, I became overwhelmed by the enormity of the decision we made. Not frightened or alarmed, but simply awestruck.

Somehow God gives us certain parents, certain relatives, and certain siblings, and these people become our family. We did not choose them. But a husband is different. He's a man that you actually choose out of a cast of millions. What an awesome feat! I actually picked this man out of all the men walking on the planet. He will become the most significant part of my family—my husband, the man I will share my hopes and dreams with until death do we part. In all my crazy life I had never made such an important decision. Yet I wonder, did I really pick Mark, or did God pick him for me?

As the minister was reading our vows, I looked into your dad's eyes and I knew I had picked the right man. He is perfect for me. Not perfect, mind you, just perfect for me. Certainly he has his faults, as I have mine. Just like everyone else, we will have to work at our marriage to make it stronger as the years go by.

And all of that hard work to come was condensed into a brief second as the Hawaiian minister gently nudged me back to reality. Apparently it was my turn to say "I do."

The next day those words "I do" kept ringing in my ears. Yes, I do love him, and I do commit myself to him, and I do honor him. But more than just that, I do respect him, I do trust him, and I do admire his integrity and his kind heart. And lucky me, because now he is my husband! Sure there are hard times, and there are problems. We are alive, therefore we struggle—but we do it together.

I am hopeful that your wedding day may be one of the most precious days of your life! Lord knows that every day is precious, but my prayer for you is that on this day you can look into your husband's eyes and feel the same love, respect, and trust that I felt for your dad on the day we were married.

Enjoy your new life together, Carly. I wish you and your husband all the happiness and love in the world.

> *Love,*
> *Mom*

I enclosed a photo from our wedding, sealed the letter, and wrote "To open on your wedding day" on the back. I put it out in our mailbox and lifted the flag so it would be postmarked that day. It was mailed to our home address and said "Mom" in the corner.

The next day it was delivered back to me with the postal seal and date on it. I put it away with the other letters in Carly's letter box.

I heard the other day that the postal carrier wondered if I had realized what I was doing. Why on earth would anyone mail a letter to someone at their own house? She was convinced it was a mistake. I thought nothing would surprise them.

FALL

We flew back to California after the wedding, but the dream house on the North Shore of Oahu is calling our name. Mark has long intended for Hawaii to be his home. On Carly's first birthday we packed our belongings and moved.

Although I had visited the house before, when we opened the door and stepped inside, it felt different. It is no longer a place to go for vacations, it is home.

The first night we put Carly to bed earlier than usual. The time change was in our favor, so Mark and I sat on the deck in the backyard and watched the pounding surf.

"How does it feel to be here?" asked Mark. He held my hand.

"This moment it feels great. I'm already relaxed. This has been a crazy year. I feel like a washing machine that's been on a constant spin cycle."

"Well, you should be nice and dizzy," joked Mark.

"Yeah, but I just want to soak for a while." Mark then reassured me that I was in the right place for "soaking" and maybe even some "floating," even though this was a big change for me. He had certainly gone out of his way to prepare the house for our arrival, including everything from a house full of tropical flowers to fences and all the safety precautions necessary for a small child living on the beach.

I am thankful I arrived before my boxes; it has given me time to adjust.

It's an odd feeling, moving into another woman's life. I cook with her pots and pans and season our food with her spices. I sleep on her side of the bed and use her shampoo and bath towels. It feels like I have given up my own familiar life and now I am intruding on someone else's. This is by no means apparent to Mark, but it's a bigger adjustment than I expected.

The most challenging moment came last week. We had kept ourselves busy for days getting Carly's room ready and filling the house with groceries and other essentials. We returned home one day and there they were, a large box for Carly and three others for me. I had been living out of a suitcase until that day, eagerly awaiting the arrival of my clothes.

It didn't fully sink in until I saw those boxes. Then it hit me: all of Ronnie's things were still hanging in the closet.

Last year, Mark and a couple of Ronnie's best friends had packed up all of her clothes and toiletries in their California house. It took an entire day, and it had been terribly difficult for Mark.

So there we were, in a different closet in a different place and time. Mark and I walked upstairs and looked inside. There were years of life and experiences neatly folded in those drawers and hanging brightly from the wooden racks.

Mark apologized. "Sorry I haven't gotten to this yet."

"That's OK. I know this is a tough one for you."

"Yeah, it's just so final. Last time it took forever, and I had friends to help me."

"I'll help you. I can even do it myself if you don't want to go through it all again."

Mark hugged me tight.

We agreed that I would get started with the obvious stuff and that when Mark returned we would finish the task together.

As I always assume I can handle anything, I dove right in. I decided to begin with the drawers. Mark would return to no major changes, and I would be making progress. Quietly and alone, I stepped into the closet. Instantly Ronnie came to life for me. It's been a year and a half since her passing, but at that moment I felt so strongly the presence of the woman who walked in those dresses.

Eventually, I opened the top dresser drawer. Underwear. "Can I do this?" I asked myself. This was a job that required assistance from my best friend.

Debrah answered the phone and I immediately started talking.

"OK. I'm standing in Ronnie's closet, which is apparently now my closet. I need to move my things in, which also involves moving her things out. I'm not sure if I'm up for this."

Deb always calls me Dee. She likes solutions, just like Mark. "OK, this is what you need to do." I knew directions would follow. "Start with the T-shirts. Then go to socks and accessories. Work your way to underwear and call me later."

"Thanks, Deb." I hung up with a plan, which made venturing into this uncomfortable and personal territory easier to face.

T-shirts and socks were easy. From there, I went through drawers of accessories and trinkets that I knew her sister would love to have. I set her earrings aside for Mark to look at. I packed up purses, belts, shoes, and shirts. Suddenly I found myself back at the underwear drawer.

Going through it wasn't too difficult at all until the moment I discovered that her underwear was tiny and her bras were way bigger than I thought they'd be. "Can this get any harder?" I asked myself.

I called Deb back. "I am such a girl," I said as soon as she answered.

"What do you mean? How's it going?"

"Well, let's just say I thought I was doing a pretty decent job of not feeling jealous of Mark's perfect first wife until right now."

"Why, what happened? Is it the closet thing?" Deb asked.

"It's the underwear thing," I admitted with a slight moan in my voice. "It's just much, much harder going through someone else's life than I thought it would be."

Deb clearly wasn't used to hearing me sound so insecure. "Just keep it up, Dee. You're almost done, and then you can get settled. What a year you guys have had, but just think about it, now you have each other and your life together is really about to begin." She is always so encouraging.

"I know, Deb, you're right. I just want to soak for a while."

"You'll get there soon," she reassured me, as if she had heard my analogy the night before.

Carly's adjustment to her new surroundings is a task she takes seriously. She's determined to explore every item in every box, drawer, and cabinet in the house, and her exploits prepare us all for a nice long nap each day. The other day, when she was sleeping soundly in her crib, Mark and I poked our heads into her room. We watched her sleep for a minute, her little chest raising up and down with every peaceful breath. Mark whispered in my ear, "She is just the sweetest angel."

The next day, when Carly was in an exaggerated moment of pure frustration, I looked over at Mark and asked, "How can someone who's only two-foot-four possibly be so demanding?"

He laughed and said, "Just wait. Someday she'll be five-foot-four."

Some of my most priceless memories are the quiet times that Mark and I spent together just staring at her smiling face.

There's something about Hawaii. It's a fertile place. Some say it's the weather; others say it's the water. Personally, I think it's the relaxed atmosphere, especially where we live on the North Shore. There are children everywhere, lots of them. It's old-fashioned family-style living, like I would imagine our grandparents used to live.

We've been here only five weeks, and we have just discovered a new baby is already on the way. Maybe it's the water. Mark is so excited I think he walked around with tears in his eyes for two full days.

This is a wonderful neighborhood, but settling into a small town has its disadvantages as well. People are curious about almost everything. We've been doing some gardening, and there was a pile of dirt near the front of our house. This afternoon three different people stopped to ask us what the pile of dirt was for.

We started making up different answers.

"It's an escape tunnel."

"It's a burial ground for ex-boyfriends."

"It's a neighborhood ant farm."

Actually, it's a pile of dirt.

Twila, my neighbor down the street, has told me about the stir Mark and I created the first time I visited here while I was still very pregnant.

I can understand the curiosity. The people in Hawaii reacted differently. Ronnie died in California, we had lots of friends in common there, and people had seen us together for months. But Mark's friends and neighbors on the North Shore hadn't seen him much since Ronnie died, and then he shows up one day with me, and I was eight months pregnant.

Every morning, I would go swimming and snorkeling in the ocean for exercise. I would swim in one direction and then return home on the beach. Apparently the neighbors were anxious to get a glimpse of me and my huge stomach, and according to Twila, the coconut telegraph was burning up the wires when I passed from house to house.

"Mark's new pregnant girlfriend is walking down the beach, check her out." Thank goodness I had no idea.

At least I can laugh with Twila over that one now.

Our son, Jackson, had a rough time entering this world. During delivery his heart rate dropped dramatically. Four doctors and a nurse were in the delivery room, and for a few silent moments they were all standing still watching the equipment that monitored his heart rate.

I was frightened. Our son was in danger and timing was critical. The doctors were unsure why he would not come out, but they said I should give it all I had. We needed to hurry.

Jack was born, but he was blue and the umbilical cord was wrapped around his neck two times. Our doctor said it was a miracle that he made it out naturally, without a C-section, since the cord was wrapped so tight. Quickly his color changed to a healthy pink and he began to cry. We all cried too.

I thanked God that Jack had made it, and I also thanked God for sparing Mark the pain and agony of losing another unborn child. That would have been too much.

We returned home from the hospital with our car loaded with flowers and our new son.

The next morning he was sleeping in his daddy's arms. The look of love in Mark's eyes was simply beautiful. It's amazing how you fall so immediately in love with a new baby. Every finger and toe is a miracle. I counted them all twice and then stared at each little part of his face for a very long time.

I went to my desk drawer and picked out some stationery with a border of tiny blue footprints. I grabbed my favorite pen, sat down, and wrote a letter to Jack, the beginning of his letter box.

By now we've settled into our new routine. Carly loves Jack, who she assumes is a new toy, some amazing reward for good behavior. She enjoys tugging on his ears and poking him all over his tiny body. She was the first one to make him smile, so he must like it.

Early this morning, the whole family went down to the beach for a breakfast picnic. For me, this is always the calmest and most peaceful time of day to go to the beach. I was holding Jack while Carly was digging for sand crabs right next to us.

I looked at Mark, and by the faraway look on his face, I couldn't tell if he was happy or sad.

"Are you OK?" I asked.

"Yeah, I'm good," he said as he put his arm around me. "This may sound strange, but I was just wishing Ronnie could be here to meet the kids."

With a proud smile he looked over at Carly digging in the sand. Then he looked at Jack and said, "She would have loved them."

The way I live my own life has greatly improved because of Ronnie. It's odd, because I didn't know her well, but the lessons from her life and death have had a profound impact on my everyday life. Her gift to me is a deeper understanding of how to love and be loved. Since the phone call when I first heard about Ronnie's death, I have rarely looked back with regret for my life and the unexpected changes I have encountered along the way. I have learned to be content without trying to predict the ending to my story. In the case of life and death, the ending writes itself.

There are others who have also touched my life as Ronnie did. Most of them are still alive today, and it occurred to me recently that I have not always taken the time to tell them. I am thankful to those who have raised me, educated me, loved me, listened to me, mentored me, been patient with me, and showed me the way. Some of them don't even know the difference they have made. Ronnie has motivated me to share my heart with others while I still can, which I have learned to do with just a simple letter from my heart.

I also have seen the pain that remains in the hearts of those left behind after a loved one dies, but now I have found a special way to share my love forever, whether I am alive or not. Inside my letter box is a legacy of love, and I see clearly now that even the letter box is a gift from Ronnie.

Today, I was inspired to write what may appear to be a sad letter. The reason for this letter is also part of the gift that Ronnie left. We will all leave a legacy when we die, of this we may be certain. I imagine that our everyday experiences will be memorable to those who knew us, the obvious results of the seeds we have planted on our walk along the road toward heaven.

But who will know our heart if we don't take the time to share it? Our feelings are left to the interpretation of those around us, even in life, but especially in death. I don't want the message in my heart to be left for those I love to only imagine. I want them to know that if I could, I would proclaim my love for them for today, for tomorrow, and for eternity.

Today I am writing for a time in the future. I am writing about death, but I am certainly not sick. I am alive and healthy, and I stand in awe of the capacity for one heart to love so greatly.

To open upon my death

My dearest children,

As you can imagine, this is the most difficult letter for me to write. Right now, as I contemplate death, it is not fear of dying that causes me pain but rather the thought of leaving my family behind.

When I was younger, I was always so grateful for living, but I was also so curious about why we are here and where we were going after this part of our journey ends. I spent hours thinking about the meaning of life and, in particular, what was I doing here. Of course, I never had any answers to these age-old questions, so I would end my internal philosophy lesson with the feeling that there must be something more besides this existence on earth. Part of me could not wait to find out what that was.

I suppose I can dig deep down and still find that feeling, but something drastically changed in me after I married your dad and started our family.

For the first time I planted roots. I mean emotional roots. The kind of roots that attach you to another human being and are so strong that they stretch to the far corners of the earth.

I can remember being afraid to love your dad as much as I did. I thought love was like this mathematical equation. The amount that a heart loves is in direct proportion to the amount that a heart can feel pain. As I grew more deeply in love, I was acutely aware of how painful it would be to lose him.

And then you children came along. That bond is so different. It was solid from the second you were born. Life began to make more sense to me, and I could not imagine life without my family.

Every year, every day, every moment is a gift. I have been blessed with many wonderful memories that bring a smile to my face or tears of happiness to my eyes. I have also struggled and suffered, and I remember those times as well with a smile on my face, because in the end, so far, every struggle has helped form the person that I am.

As I think about my own death—and my own life—
I keep coming back to that mathematical equation
about love. The pleasure of knowing and giving love is
what really matters on earth. And I feel content. I have
felt love and I continue to feel love every moment of
every day.

I may not be the richest, most beautiful, or healthiest per-
son. Considering the size of this planet, I may not know
very many people intimately and deeply. And God knows
I have not suffered or felt the deep pain that many others
have in this lifetime. So, was my life worth it? Did I make
a difference? Did I laugh and cry through the years? And
most importantly, did I know love?

Yes, yes, yes. And I pray that in your lifetime, you, too,
will experience all the pleasure and pain that life brings
you with open arms. This way, you will also leave this
earth with a full heart.

I can only imagine this to be a difficult time for you as
well. Find strength in your faith. Let our fond memories
comfort you now. We have had so much. You have given
me so much. Now your outgoing spirit and your generous

heart will fill you with the desire to go on to live a won-
derful life and to share your gifts with others.

I will close with this, my dears. As you get older, I pray
that your life will be filled with people and love. Make
loving one another your priority, for as I have heard
many times before, when that final day comes, you will
not be concerned with how much money is in your bank
account or how successful you were in business. You will
only care about the people you love and the wonderful
memories of times spent with them. So, please take the
time to cultivate those memories and you will reap the
harvest of life's sweetest fruit.

I have enjoyed each and every moment of this life with
you. I can still remember the first moment I saw your
face and held you in my arms. My memories are filled
with your sweet smiles and your chunky tears and every-
thing in between. I will remember you and everything
about you.

Although I will miss you greatly, I believe that someday
we will be together again. On that day I will look into

those sweet eyes to thank you once again for bringing
more joy to my life than I could have ever imagined.

So until that day, good-bye.

> *I love you,*
> *Mom*

Ⓓ

Wednesdays are date night, complete with adult conversation and dinner. We recently decided to make them more interesting by trying some different activities together. Last week we went fishing for little Hawaiian bait-fish, and Mark thought that was the perfect date. This week, it was my turn.

After three trips from the car to unload our things, we set up our cooler and other essentials on the warm sand at Waimea Bay, about twenty minutes from our home.

"Is this really date night or is this some weeklong adventure you have planned?" Mark asked with a sarcastic grin.

"Honey, I promise someday you will come to appreciate my planning skills—maybe not tonight, but someday." He didn't look convinced.

"You got any hula dancers in there?" He couldn't control himself.

We went swimming and snorkeling until sunset. We saw many colorful fish and eels, and Mark even saw a small shark. I'm sure at that moment he was thankful I had packed his fins.

Later, we poured glasses of wine and watched the sun set into the ocean. We had a wonderful picnic, and as the night air became cool we cuddled close into each other's arms.

"Let's have another baby." His words came from nowhere.

"Now," I responded, for lack of anything better to say.

"Well, soon. Let's have another baby soon. Then they'll all be close in age and we can do more together when they are young. And then they'll be close when they grow up. And besides, you make such beautiful babies. What do you think?"

When Mark owned his company, they often used a hand gesture that constituted absolute agreement with no turning back. It meant a final decision had been made and everyone had taken ownership of it. You simply take your clenched fist and "bonk" yourself on the forehead. Everyone has to agree, or it isn't valid.

We talked for the rest of the evening about the idea of having a third child. Before we packed up our things to head home, we bonked on it.

The following week we found out I was already pregnant.

This pregnancy has not been fun. The nausea is indeed nauseating. The mood swings have been epic. But it is the insomnia that has been most unbearable. There have been very few nights, especially as we get near the end, that I sleep more than three or four hours. And then a couple of fully-charged, die-hard batteries wake up promptly at 5 A.M., run down the hall, and grace Mark and me with their presence.

On one occasion, after being up all night, I decided to take a bath at about 3 A.M. I added half of a jar of my favorite aromatherapy bath milk and managed to relax so much I woke up two hours later in an ice-cold tub with my head part way in the water.

I must say, I am grateful the kids woke up or I might have drowned, and that would have been just too much for Mark to deal with. I can see the headlines now: "Pregnant woman drowns in bathtub from aromatherapy overdose."

The week before Hannah was born, I was getting desperate. My doctor said she was ready, but she just wouldn't come out. I called my next-door neighbor, "Della, can you come down to Twila's with me? We can walk down with the kids."

"Sure," said Della. She's always ready to go.

On the way to Twila's, I revealed my mission. I had a plan. If anything would help me go into labor it would be this.

"No way," said Della. "This, I've got to see."

We made it to Twila's front yard with me waddling the entire way. The kids followed behind, imitating me like a flock of baby ducks. Today, the kids would have to wait to get on the trampoline. It was my idea and I was first. The kids ran for cover. Passing cars honked, waved, and drove by slowly to get a good glimpse of me bouncing up and down.

My doctor has a picture of this undignified event hanging on the wall in her office with a joke underneath that says, "If this won't induce labor, nothing will!" It's true, it didn't help me at all, but a week later Hannah Lee Button was born. This birth was actually fun and easy, and every difficult moment from the months before vanished the second I saw her face.

I love our first family photo. Mark is beaming with his arm around all of us. Time alone doesn't heal wounds—it takes love, too.

Ⓓ

Having kids has brought out a refreshing piece of our hearts that we rarely saw in each other before. In some ways, we hadn't even seen them in ourselves for many years. I think they were lying dormant somewhere between the responsibility gene and the career gene. It's the easy-going playful gene that knows deep down that we never really have to grow up.

One recent sunny afternoon the Hawaiian sky decided to bless us with a beautiful tropical downpour. We were just leaving the house and Mark asked me to grab an umbrella.

"Umbrella?" I questioned him, as if he were an alien. "You want me to bring an umbrella?"

"Yeah, it's pouring," he informed me, as if I had no idea.

"Well, sorry, but I don't own an umbrella. I don't like them. To me, they are a sign of aging, and not the good kind.

"Besides," I continued, "don't you love to play in the rain? Come on. Let's go." I tucked my arm into his and pulled him outside.

"I think our friends were right. Maybe we got married too soon," Mark joked.

"Isn't there anything you like to do that reminds you of being a kid?" I asked him. "Like jumping in puddles?"

We walked down the street in the rain to our neighbor's house. Mark and I spent half an hour looking at all the rainbow colors and reflections and then jumping in the puddles along the road.

"I'm a fun guy, you know. You just haven't had the opportunity to see that part of me yet," Mark tried to convince me.

"That's because we're just finally getting a chance to play," I assured him.

We returned home looking like we had just come in from an afternoon swim with our clothes on. We made hot chocolate, a rare event in Hawaii, and then rolled on the floor and tickled each other until we cried.

I knew right then and there that Mark had indeed remembered how to laugh. It must have pleased Ronnie, as it certainly did me, to see that Mark's spirit had found its way back.

MARK

SIX YEARS HAVE PASSED SINCE THAT unforgettable spring day that I lost my first wife. I have learned since then that we are indeed given second chances in life, but we must dig deep within to find the strength and courage to seek them out. It doesn't always make sense, and that is where faith and trust become important. I may never truly understand why Ronnie had to die when she was so very young and alive. But God knows, and in this I have found peace.

What I believe to be true is that there is a beloved and loving dark-haired angel with three bouncing babies watching over me every moment from above.

What I see right now is that there is a beautiful woman with three sweet children playing out in the backyard. I hear them calling me now: "Daddy, come play with us."

Your Own Letter Box

PART TWO

MARK & DIANE

Dear Friends,

Now you know the story of how we first created our letter boxes and how we have made them part of our lives as future gifts to our children. When we first started telling people about the idea, everyone was immediately intrigued, and many began to create boxes for their own loved ones. We have included this section of the book to help those of you who may wish to do the same.

We feel that one of the strengths of the "Letter Box" idea lies in its simplicity: It's for anyone who has loved deeply and who wants to preserve that tie for generations to come. Whether directed to a friend, mentor, or family member, the acts of expressing and sharing that love are inherently enriching for all involved. Letter boxes are for all parents who have felt the incomparable bond between themselves and their children and who dream about watching them grow from bouncing babies through adulthood, cherishing every memory in between.

As the years have passed, we have continued writing to our children, and now Carly, Jack, and Hannah each have a letter box. Over time we have gathered together a collection of letters expressing our deepest feelings, thoughts, and hopes for the future to encourage them through life. Each letter has been mailed, postmarked, and safely stored away, to be opened at a certain significant moment in their respective lives. Besides the loving support we provide our children each day, we believe that these letters are one of the most valuable gifts they will receive from us. Their letter boxes are our lifelong connection to them, time taken to ensure that important words have not been left unspoken.

In our own lives, loved ones have already left us, taking with them thoughts and feelings we will never know. Maybe you, too, have lost a parent, grandparent, aunt, friend, or other loved one. Wouldn't opening a letter written years ago by the hand of that person be an incomparable gift? Wouldn't you cherish forever their words of love, wisdom, and faith? Such a letter might bring back beautiful memories or perhaps reveal something important about that person which you never knew before. Perhaps just a simple expression of love before the signature would be a treasure in itself.

The Letter Box is our invitation for you to cast your own legacy into the hearts of those you treasure. Don't worry about grammar or punctuation, and don't wait to get started. Our time on earth is precious and uncertain, consisting of lessons, sacrifices, challenges, successes, failures, highs, lows, and a whole lot more. Tell your story. Share your heart. It will be a testament to both your mortality and immortality—a legacy that endures for generations.

We believe you are a special and important link in a very long chain.

With love,
Mark & Diane Button

Getting Started on your Letter Box

1. Write a letter for a particular occasion, to be opened now or in the future. On some occasions, you may wish to ask another special person to write a letter or note to include with yours.

2. Add photos or other special memorabilia such as newspaper clippings, world statistics, grocery receipts, magazine articles, quotes, cartoons, or any other interesting memorabilia. You may choose to personalize your stationery with stickers, stamps, calligraphy, art, or drawings.

3. Seal the letter, specify the occasion it should be opened on the envelope, and (if possible) mail it, "care of" yourself at your own address. Remember, for those letters that will be opened in the future, the postmark and stamp mark their places in history.

4. Finally, look for a box or album to keep your letters in, such as an old cigar box. You may want to try your hand at making one yourself, turning an ordinary box into a special one.

5. Have fun!

Tips to Make Your
Letters Last a Lifetime

1 Since these letters may be sealed for decades, it is important to choose permanent markers and pens. Plain ink may dull over time, so we recommend fade-resistant, waterproof ink. Craft stores carry a variety of these in different colors and tip styles. Be creative.

2 Paper should be acid-free so it will withstand the test of time. Higher pH paper may crack or deteriorate over the years; it may also damage your photographs.

3 Glue should be permanent as well. Ask a craft-store retailer for the kinds that are used by library archivists.

4 You may wish to archive your letters in your computer or make copies to store in a separate place. As your collection grows, this testament of your love for your friends and family will likely become one of your most cherished possessions.

Tips for Letter Writing

We all want to know that we are loved. Each letter box is a golden opportunity to create a legacy of love and to guarantee that a piece of your heart lives on. Whichever way you choose to convey your deepest feelings to those you care about, the most important thing is to get them down on paper. Don't be afraid to show the real you. Those who are dear to you will love you and accept you, flaws and all. Share your memories of your own past as well as memories that include the person for whom the letter is intended. Children will want to know about things they did and family adventures they may not remember. Parents, friends, or mentors will be touched to learn how special they are to you. Be lavish with praise, generous with your heart, but above all, write from a place of love.

THOUGHTFUL QUESTIONS FOR YOUR LETTER BOX LETTERS

The questions on the following pages are provided as a springboard from which to start your letter writing. We hope they remind you of meaningful experiences you may have forgotten or of sides of yourself you may not often think about but would enjoy sharing in your letters.

Keep in mind that not every question is intended for any one person who reads this book. The questions about giving marital advice won't necessarily help an unmarried reader; the questions about reflecting back on old age won't help a young one. Ignore the questions that don't apply to you; there are plenty of thought-provoking questions for everyone.

For a graduation, or any successfully completed program of study

• Where did you go to school and why? If you didn't go to college, what do you consider the most educational experience you've ever had?

• How did your education, formal or otherwise, change your personality or the way you view the world?

• If you have experienced a formal learning environment, what was the best part? What was your favorite subject or course?

• What was the most difficult part? What was your least favorite subject or course?

• Where did you live during your "learning years"? What did you eat?

• What did you do for fun during this time? What sports and activities were you involved in? What music did you listen to?

• Were there any teachers or friends who became a mentor or role model to you? Who taught you the most? Did you like or respect that person? Did you ever receive help from someone you didn't fully appreciate until later?

• What advice would you give your letter's recipient as he or she enters the work force and adjusts to a new life?

• How has your education or training contributed to your success in life?

• What did you "always want to be when you grew up"? Did that dream change? Are you glad about it? Regretful?

For difficult times

• What was the most difficult situation you have ever encountered?

• How did you handle it? How did you feel?

• What emotions do you show easily? Which ones do you hide? Do you wish you could share more or less than you do?

• What is your philosophy about pain and suffering? Why do you believe humans suffer so much?

• Has any person or group of people helped you through a particularly tough time? Who?

• Have any of your beliefs helped you heal? Explain how.

• What saying or thought has given you comfort and strength that you would like to pass on to the person who receives this letter?

• Are your feelings easily hurt? Do you place importance on what others think of you?

• Have you learned any valuable life lessons through the trials in your life? What?

• What regrets do you have? What do you do in your present life to cope with these feelings? What do you do now to avoid making similar mistakes?

• What have you learned about yourself from the mistakes you have made? Have you changed? What are you still working to change?

FOR WHEN SOMEONE FALLS IN LOVE

• When was the first time you fell in love? How old were you? Was this the person you married?

• Where did you go on your first date with this person? When and where was your first kiss?

• What did falling in love feel like the first time?

• Who do you know who has a "love" relationship you admire?

• What does love mean to you?

• Who is your love now? Do you feel better about yourself with this person in your life?

• Did you fall in love immediately or did it grow over time? Were you "best friends" first?

• How did you know you were falling in love? Were you always staring at each other or could you see your unborn children in your partner's eyes?

• What was the most fun thing you ever did with this person? Did you laugh often? Do you still laugh often?

• What do you feel is the secret to keeping the spark alive in a relationship? Have you ever fallen out of love? Could it have been avoided?

For a wedding day

• How did you meet your spouse? What were your first impressions? Did you have a lot in common?

• How long did you date? Why did you fall in love? What qualities did your spouse have that you admired? Are these the same things you admire now?

• What did you believe marriage would be like? What were your concerns? How has it been different than you expected?

• What do you remember most about your wedding day?

• Where did you go on your honeymoon?

• How did you feel about the family you were marrying into?

• What advice would you give the recipient of this letter as he or she takes this important step? About love? About commitment? About the struggles? About making the bond last?

• What was the first year of your marriage like? Do you remember a special day or weekend you spent together during the first year? What do you do for fun together now?

• What is the most difficult part about being married? How do you handle the conflict?

• What is the best part about being married? What do you love most about your spouse now?

For the birth of a child

• Describe the months you (or your partner) were pregnant. How did you feel emotionally and physically?

• Who attended the birth? Were they helpful?

• How was the delivery? Was it in a hospital, at home, or elsewhere?

• How did you feel the first time you saw your baby?

• Who was there to help in the beginning? Family? Friends and neighbors?

• Who chose your child's name? How was the decision made? What were the other possibilities?

• What were you like as a new parent? Were you surprised by your attitudes or parenting styles? Did you and your partner have conflicting thoughts about how to raise children?

• What was the biggest challenge as a new parent? What was your favorite part?

• How has your life changed from this experience?

• What would you like the recipient of this letter to keep in mind as a new parent?

FOR ANY WINTER HOLIDAY CELEBRATION

• How did you spend your most memorable holiday? Where were you? Who were you with?

• What are your family traditions? What were the holidays like when you were a child? Who do you associate with the holidays who is now gone but who you would like the person who gets this letter to know about?

• Do you have a favorite holiday song, story, or play?

• What does the holiday season mean to you? What would you like the recipient of this letter to remember about these gatherings right now or in the future?

• What was the best holiday gift you have ever received? Who gave it to you and why did it mean so much? What was the best holiday gift you have ever given?

• Do you go to any religious services during the holidays? Where?

• How do you decorate your home?

• Have you ever been away from loved ones during the holiday season? What was the cause? Where were you? How did it feel?

• What was the coldest winter you can ever remember? Or the warmest? What did you do? Where were you?

• What do you and your family usually eat during the holidays? Do you cook? What is your favorite dish?

FOR ANY VALENTINE'S DAY

• How did you spend your most memorable Valentine's Day? Who were you with?

- What does Valentine's Day mean to you?

- Do you have any Valentine's Day traditions?

- What is your idea of a "perfect" Valentine's Day?

- How do you make the one you love feel special?

- Is romance an important part of your life?

- What is the most romantic thing someone could do for you on Valentine's Day?

- Do you remember your first Valentine? Who was it? What did this person do to make you feel special?

- Was Valentine's Day a special day in your family when you were a child? What did you do?

- How would you define the word *love* to someone?

FOR A WEDDING ANNIVERSARY

- If you are married, how do you spend your wedding anniversaries? Do you have any traditions?

- Do you always remember your anniversary? Does your spouse? Have either of you ever forgotten?

• How many years have you been married? How did you celebrate your first anniversary?

• How has your love grown or changed over the years? Are you closer now or when you were first married?

• Do you enjoy spending time together? What hobbies, interests, and activities do you have in common?

• What is the best advice you could give the person who gets this letter to learn and understand about marriage as the years go by?

• What do you love, appreciate, and respect most about your spouse?

• Looking back over your family history, did couples stay married for life or were there many divorces? What do you do to make your marriage work?

• Who else have you known with a loving and inspirational marriage? Why? What seems to make it work?

• When you remember marrying your spouse, what was the reason you chose this particular person? Do you still love the same things about your spouse that you did in the beginning? Why?

FOR A LOVED ONE AFTER YOUR DEATH

• Who have you loved deeply in your life?

• What are your spiritual beliefs? How do they affect your thoughts about death?

• What do you look forward to or fear about death?

• From your own perspective, has your life been a success?

• Have you ever left anything unsaid that you now regret? What would you like to say to the recipient of this letter that you've never been able to say before?

• What have you cherished most in life?

• What has been the greatest lesson you have ever learned?

• What motto or philosophy has helped get you through life's challenges?

• What was your happiest, saddest, or most special memory?

• How do you want to be remembered?

- How did this person first come into your life?

- What qualities, talents, or gifts does this person have that you admire most?

- Why is this person special to you?

- What specific thing did this person say or do that changed your life? Did it happen over time or in one sudden epiphany?

- What have you learned from your experience with this person?

- How have you applied what he or she taught you to your life?

- Have you, in turn, been able to pass this wisdom on to others?

- How are you different because of the effect this person had on your life? How often do you reflect on what this person taught you?

• Is there anything specific that always reminds you of your teacher or mentor?

• What would you like the world to know about this person? What would you like this person to know about how much he or she has meant to you?

For someone you want to thank

• Why are you grateful to this person?

• What did this gesture mean to you? How did you feel when you received it?

• How has your life changed because of this person?

• How different might your life be if not for this person and the impact they had on you?

• Have you gone on to help others as a result of this person's generosity? What have you done? Who have you helped?

• How would you describe this person to others?

• When did you first meet this person? What was your first impression of him or her?

- What qualities make this person stand out?

- What are your thoughts about giving?

- How will this person's gift affect your life in the future? How did it affect the future of others?

For healing broken relationships

- What are some special qualities you admire about this person? What do you miss about your relationship? Can you remember any good times?

- How has your life been different without this person? How have you changed? How would your relationship be different today?

- Why did you choose this point in time to write this letter?

- Are you ready to make amends and begin healing?

- Would you like this person to be a part of your life again? Why? If not, what would you desire the outcome to be?

- If you could say only one thing, one sentence, to this person, what would you say?

• If you could go back in time and change the situation, what would you do differently?

• Can you take responsibility for any mistakes you may have made? If appropriate, can you apologize and ask for forgiveness? Can you forgive yourself?

• Have you forgiven past mistakes this person may have made that hurt you? Are you willing to let go of the past and begin anew?

• With peace and love as your goals, what do you want to say?

FOR A DEAR FRIEND

• When did you first become friends? How did your friendship grow?

• Why is this person your friend? When did your relationship turn the corner from acquaintances to friends and then to close friends?

• What qualities does he or she have that are special for you?

• What was the best advice your friend has ever given you? Did you take it to heart? Did you benefit from it?

• How has your friend changed your life? How would your life be different if that person wasn't there?

• What challenges has your friendship withstood? Have you ever had a falling out and patched things up again?

• Does this friend know things about you that no one else does? What? Is there any secret you have never shared with this friend that you would like to? Can you share it now? Why haven't you mentioned it before?

• When have you been the most appreciative of this person's friendship?

• Was there a time when this friend supported you that you have never forgotten?

• What do you value most about your friendship? Is there anything you would change if you could? How do you anticipate your friendship to be in the future? What are you looking forward to?

• What is your fondest memory of this friend?

• What were your dreams and goals at this time in your own life? What did you most look forward to?

• Were you confident? Optimistic? Pessimistic?

• Were you close to your parents and family? How has your relationship with them changed since then?

• Who were your best friends?

• Where did you live? Did you enjoy this place?

• What was the best part of life during your twenties? What was the most difficult? What would you encourage the person who receives this letter to think about as he or she enters adulthood?

• What were your spiritual beliefs? Have they changed? Did you go to church or temple?

• Did you have any special talents or "gifts"? What were they?

• What kind of music did you listen to? Who were your favorite artists? Did you dance? Did you play any musical instruments? Which ones?

• What did you do for fun on the weekends? Did you exercise or participate in any other activities or groups? What were they?

• What was the most exhilarating or vivid moment of your thirties?

• How would you have described yourself then? If you are old enough to look back at this age, what would you now say about yourself at thirty?

• What are your best qualities? What about the not-so-great ones?

• What style of clothing do you wear? Do you consider yourself to be fashionable?

• What are your three favorite foods? What items do you always have in your refrigerator?

• Do you enjoy sports and exercise? Which ones do you participate in regularly?

• How have you changed as a person since you were young? How has the world changed?

• Who or what do you appreciate most in life? What would you encourage the person who will receive this letter to savor most in his or her life at this age?

• What are your plans for the next decade? What excites you most in your life?

• What is the best advice you have ever received?

FOR A FORTIETH BIRTHDAY

• How did you feel about hitting the big four-oh? How did you feel physically? Emotionally? If you haven't turned forty yet, what do you expect life to be like at this time?

• If you are there already, what surprised you about being in your forties?

• Is a sense of community important to you? Politics? What do you believe about giving back and charity in general?

• Are you in a career that you enjoy? What is your philosophy about work?

• What is your philosophy about money? How do you feel about your own financial situation?

• Who are the most special people in your life? Why?

• What goals and dreams have you accomplished in your life? What have been your biggest disappointments?

• What have you come to feel is the most important thing in life? How can the person to whom you are writing this letter learn from your knowledge and experience?

• What has changed the most in your life or in society over the past decade?

• What are you looking forward to doing with the rest of your life?

FOR A FIFTIETH BIRTHDAY

• Did turning fifty feel like a special milestone to you? What did it mean?

• What is the greatest success of your life so far? What is the greatest failure? What obstacles have you overcome in your lifetime?

• What was the best vacation you ever took? Who was with you? Where do you still want to go?

• Who are the most important people in your life? Who do you call when you need support?

• What was the funniest moment you can remember in your life? What happened? Who were you with? Do you have a favorite joke?

• What regret do you have that could have been avoided? What advice can you give your letter's recipient about living life in the most rewarding and satisfying way possible?

• What is the greatest book you have ever read? Who is your favorite author? Do you have a favorite song or movie?

• What was your most embarrassing moment?

• What is your favorite season of the year? Why?

• If you hadn't chosen the career or path in life you did, what career would you have wanted to choose?

• What possessions and personal belongings are important to you now? What no longer seems important that once did?

• What is the best idea you have ever had?

• What does "security" mean to you?

• What were the biggest fears in your life? What are your fears now? What would you advise the recipient of this letter to not worry about?

• Do you remember yourself as a child? What are some of your first memories? Do you still have any of those "child-like" qualities? What are they?

• In retrospect, what was the happiest time of your life? What was the saddest?

• What is the most challenging thing you have ever had to do?

• What was the last unexpected or spontaneous thing you have done? Would you do it again?

• What are the most significant changes you have seen in your lifetime? In society? In technology? In our environment? In you?

• What have you been most passionate about in your life? What are you passionate about today? What are you looking forward to in the future?

• Is there any "secret" you have never shared but wanted to? Can you do it now?

Some thoughts to ponder for a variety of occasions

• Who would you choose to be if you could be any person in the history of the world?

• Who would you describe as the most influential person in history?

• What do you think is the most powerful emotion a human being can express?

- Using your own definition of the term, who is the most "beautiful" person you know?

- Who would you like to be with you when you die? What do you want to say?

- What is the closest thing to a miracle you have ever experienced or witnessed?

- What is your idea of a perfect day? What about a perfect life?

- If you could do one thing to change the world for the better, what would you do?

- Who has been the greatest role model in your life?

- What does "God" mean to you? What makes a "spiritual" person?

- If you could pray for only one thing in life, what would it be?

ACKNOWLEDGMENTS

With boundless gratitude we thank those who have walked along the path with us to make this dream come true.

First and foremost, to God, our creator and the one true author of our lives.

To our parents and our families, for your constant and loving support and guidance over the years. We love you and we thank you.

To our children, for your sweet smiles. You make it all worthwhile.

To Cindy Black, Richard Cohn, and the entire staff at Beyond Words Publishing, for seeing the heart and soul of this project and indeed inspiring us to integrity. We could not have asked for a more collaborative, resourceful, and creative team. Thank you all.

A special thanks to Jenefer Angell, our editor. You are a kind, insightful, and uncompromising word wizard.

To everyone at the Maui Writers Conference and Retreat, for creating opportunities and friendships.

To Scott Stillinger, the "real" Koosh Ball inventor, and everyone at OddzOn. You are an exceptional group of talented people.

To Ronnie's family, for wonderful and precious memories.

To Holly Perreira and Pania Robinson, for going the extra mile to keep order in our lives and food in our refrigerator.

To our cheerleaders—our many friends and mentors who have helped us through challenging times and encouraged us to share this story. That list is long and wide. It includes John Barbour, Mauna Berkov, Elizabeth Boorstein, Paul and Karen Burrous, Dave and Cathy Capper, Peter Carter, Reggie Casadei, Shelton and Nalani Choy, Diane Cirincione, Terry Codington, Kawika Dowsett, Bill and Denise Duke, Debrah Farentino, Barry and Mary Golombik, Jan Hansen-Zakin, Bro. Al Henson, Jerry Jampolsky, D'Arcy Kerrigan, Jeff and Cindy Lee, Rich Marik, Ken and Kendra Martyn, Tom Mitchell, Jamie O'Rourke, Everett and Della Peacock, David and Twila Richvalsky, George and Courtney Tidmarsh, and so many others.

To the many people who have enriched our lives and shown us that love knows no limitations and recognizes no obstacles.

If you would like to contact the authors, you can e-mail them at *theletterbox@hawaii.rr.com*. Or write them at

The Letter Box
P.O. Box 150497
San Rafael, CA 94915-0497